A
SYNONYM
FOR
HOME

A
SYNONYM
FOR
HOME

Kimberly Jarchow

poems

atmosphere press

Contents

We shake with joy, we shake with grief. What a time they have, these two housed as they are in the same body.

-Mary Oliver

Patient

Let me count the ways I have broken:

Hearts,
          but no bones.
Once, a tongue bitten nearly in half.
Tripped over shoelaces,
          but still that remains harmless.
Left foot kicked into tendonitis.
A cyst developed on the back of a knee, fluid drained
          but now a fear of needles, of salt.
Hands patient and cat-scratched too many times.
Thorns of all the picked flowers turned dead bouquets.
Swallowing the trusted knife.
A throat now a graveyard of swollen things.
Two knees hugging the memory of sunburn.
Soft feet now thick from hot desert.
The bitter aftertaste of my last name.
The haunting desire of a popped vein.
The weight I needed to keep,
          but I lost it anyway.

     And my mind went with it,
but they're both coming back to me.

Broken and Hoping

Someday came today
in the produce section of
our local Sprouts. I always
push the cart, and she lets me
follow, still, as she plans our
food for us. We've run out of
pink salt. I know her favorite
sushi, fresh in the case. On our
day off we're making stir fry
and maybe we'll use the
leftover chicken for some tacos.
It's not easy, but we're getting
there, where we need to be.
She lets me pick out the
avocados, and they're the
best we've had in weeks.
Things don't rot in the
refrigerator anymore, and
maybe I am still broken to
this body, but I am full again
hoping tomorrow will be better.
We hang the reusable shopping
bags in the pantry and unpack
all that we've done right.
for ourselves, for each other.

The Unbecoming

Clockwork beckons the nightfall
yet again, and the mirror against
                that
one   wall
falls into a shadow, a trick of light.

I unravel back down to bare skin.
Fingers reach for bra clasps,
fumbling and tugging before it falls
lifeless on the carpet.

I forget how long I can hold my breath
feel the wind of a day rush out at last.

Now the jeans, ill-fitting and undone
aggressively dragged down legs,
                kicked into a corner.
Legs starved but never thin enough
expand again, the tight indents of denim
left on desperate skin.

A thick mask's paint wiped clean
from a dirty face, still red and imperfect.

The string lights glow softly as the costume fades.

       I want so badly to call
       this place
       myself
              a home.

I face the mirror, the self-made nemesis.

After the unbecoming, I remember to be afraid, but
no amount of shedding can erase the truth that I am
the monster dissolving from my own reflection.

All The Glory

then the whole of me
wakes to new light again
    &
this cycle of forgetting forgiveness
rounds out to a softer touch
    &
let me be a prism
a spectrum of bright exhale
    &
again I want to be
amidst the alive and blooming
    &
let me slip on comfort
in loose flannel or silk
    &
uncalculated artwork yet to be
defined or crushed into downfall
    &
let me feel wild or
recklessly brand new or untethered
    &
my body hollering and begging
to stop becoming an obstacle
    &
instead this time I dance
to remember all the glory
    &
feel the sweat and taste
of summer on bare skin
    &

believe again in my worth
that it cannot weigh heavier
                                                                               &
than a good day or
the courage needed to grow

Still Colorfully Bruised

The starvation returns to consume me again,
and the fear settles along with it.
I hide under a warm darkness:
      blankets turned shelter.
dancing has dwindled back into an unsettled
spinning as the sunrise light reflects against the window.
Brittle nails run sharp through dirty hair,
      scratching my scalp.
Today is a throbbing wave, the slowest sink.
Hunger is an empty addiction:
      shaking hands pulling at skin
      a stomach filled with screaming
      purple stretch marks along thighs.
Time is a burning question mark,
      an urgent exclamation point,
      an anxious semicolon.
The sunrise is gone by now,
the shadows along the carpet
replaced by glaring daylight.

An empty body howls when it feels
the force of finally clawing out
into a harsh world, and
I, still colorfully bruised,
greet the day as if I were a fragment,
a corner of light, pushing heavily over the horizon.

Amnesia

Home used to be:

    a bad word
the haunted echo of a baby grand piano
vases full of pinecones
       (we never took root here)
waterfalls running in an untouched pool
the perfect shade of green grass
the best trimmed palm trees in the neighborhood
       (I learned growth the wrong way)
learning the sound of an engine in the driveway
empty dinners gone unnoticed
lost sunglasses and the annual summer sunburn
       (we were passed down punching bags)
the art of killing time
a sister's harsh reciprocation
midnight morse code on shared walls
       (I almost threw myself away)
chasing the pigeons off the hot tub
finding sunflowers and thinking of then
whispered threats under dusty sunsets
       (we weren't the mess they painted us to be)
drama-filled Barbie doll sessions
wishing for the worst, for amnesia
chasing all our lost yesterdays along aging asphalt
       (I never caught up to the shadow of memory
                  reflecting
              against tiny waves)

Born Again

the ghost of a lover rests easy in the doorway,
but my heart belongs to that sleepy smile already
the sunlight kissing her face to say
     good morning
and it is more than that.
the best kind of waking up to see
shadows of open doorways
leading heartbreak through and away,
only to find there is someone better
to make a home with.

I once chose the work of climbing toward the sun,
believed that this endless sweat was a labor well worth
the price, now seeing how we've already reached
the top and choose the high cliff fall instead
into cool water, into this loud splash of easy

I know better now, than to chase a girl
who never knew why she was running.
Rather, we love like an exhale, *finally*,
we can stay floating in safety, born again

I make art out of the simple curve of an eyelash,
the breeze through the screen brushing baby hairs
and find the hurt still whispering at the door
as I squeeze her hand harder, hoping
the grief will see its way out soon enough.

Grown

We will buy new mirrors when we get there.
We will find time for the beach and run
        into the water to dance with the waves.
We will dance through the month of June
        in many empty living rooms.
We will dance through the highway meadows.
We will drive through the changing skies.
We will make rearviews out of ghosts
        and salt the flaps on every cardboard box.
We will deserve our own growth and call it a living.
We will call our bodies more than reflections.
We will finish our business with time.
We will leave the Ponderosa pine trees
        to the stray cats and the ashes.
We will follow those before us.
We will unlearn the art of haunting any alley and
        call ourselves brave against the brick and mortar.
We will leave every candle burning out.
We will write poems of who we once were
        and who we hoped we could someday be.
We will be, maybe, when we get there.
We will make playlists and forget.
We will make points out of poetry.
We will make nonlinear bouquets out of hopeless fixed points.
We will find out why we are here,
        and by that I mean:

We are here because we chose to be, and a universe of stars
                                        listened.

Civil Wars

Lavender bedroom walls listened
      but never spoke.
what could they say after a door
      has already screamed?
saltwater cheeks gasped apologies
      unacceptable, dejected.
a closet buried behind two mirrors
      this is no fun house,
      but my reflection still
      birthed a monster of me.
save the dancing for the skeletons,
I am always the bad guy here.
Silence brought enemies closer:
      learn the sound of footsteps
      on stairs, the creaks of
      impending civil wars...

I know her footsteps bounding up stairs
      and fear leaves my bones.
we've all been dancing here.,
and there are no heroes,
      but we still save ourselves.
The silence here is a choice.
only the laughter of a mirror remains,
      already echoing,
she never asks for another apology from me.
swollen summer doors stay swinging wide open.
walls groan with art, and
      I become the poster child
      for sunlit post-trauma.

Crooked Limping

On my birthday, we drank cheap Moscato out of mason jars
and listened to *New Year's Day* in between
The Beatles and new age Indie.

It is the precipice of a new year together, full on future
you drink too much fireball to impress my friends
and we count down to midnight over a porcelain bowl.

I made birds out of you.
what bad luck, to greet anything new
like it's already flying away.

We forget to turn the lights off until the cats think
it is daylight, purring and scratching at our faces and
this new year already feels soft, full of bright things.

candlewax and polaroids decorated the space between us,
so let's call it like it is: a still shot fading in time.
a crooked flame with a few hours left to burn.

I want your midnights...

We've been swaying to volume turned down low
in our dimly lit apartment. You trip over your own tongue
and we collapse in laughter, limping heartbeats now
dancing toward the rest of our lives.

...but I'll be cleaning up bottles with you on New Year's Day.

Survival On Sunny Days

Two hearts collapse naked
through sweat and heavy breaths.
Waking up feeling the itch,
we lace our feet together,
a silent conversation.
The warm up is brief, more a
series of questions,
the rev of an engine.
Blankets tangle quickly, soon
brushed aside for the ease of
a smooth transition
between positions,
practiced formation of dance.
We fall apart willingly,
coming undone like shoelaces.
This is a heaven I wish to
give my whole self to,
feel the communion,
the body and the blood
and the holy ghost
all rushing through in
orgasmic cacophony.

I do sometimes believe that this is what survival looks like.

Unskippable Rocks

Here I am again:

      dancing in a sweatsuit of skin,
      showing off the thinning of me.
      I feel the music in my bones, after all.

      walking the thinnest tightrope,
      counting steps like calories
      to the point of no return.

      shaking off the dead weight,
      only pausing mere seconds
      at the protrusion of a ribcage.

If survival be the skin and sweat and pleasure of a body,
how beautiful it is to die a body emptied of water
in fear of its own waves and rippling curves.

We already know that we are sinking,
feet and hands and head like heavy stones,
jagged, unskippable rocks.

Finally, I want to unlearn the hunger,
choose less the acid, the bile,
the empty addiction,
      more the smooth of me
      growing into existence.
after all when can a home grow
if we are always downsizing?
I will no longer deny myself what is waiting to be consumed.

Still Better Than

a love that walks away
hiding in plain sight
haunted coffee shops
hating a hair color
a tie-dyed curse word
broke birthday pizza
a landslide of doubt
bleeding red rocks
a waterfall of tears
dried mud on a clean floor
a shaky come up
blown out fights
the indent of a body
on fresh green grass
shady tree pictures
a sparkling backyard
the opposite of growth
pink saturday nights
a slippery slope
every fall back down
stoking a dying fire
sand and stone
a broken record
the choice to leave
always running late
a bullet train's weight
the pop of an open chest
feeling another goodbye

Directionless Guides

We are always dancing, somehow:

three left feet
&
one right answer
&
four letter words
&
racing traffic lights
&
parking lot cars
&
driving me crazy
&
tangled hair
&
shaved eyebrows
&
clumsy two-steps
&
directionless boogies
&
maps for hearts
&
a guiding touch
&
prayers to the universe
&
the tango of passing time
&

ever interlocking fingers
        &
this movement feeling like
magic, like an old song on
the radio, like a home phone
number, like seconds counted
out in the beat of her heart.

Mornings Spent Unraveling

My addiction wipes mud into the welcome mat.
It bursts open the swollen front door
an unannounced guest, drags its baggage up
two flights up fading musty carpet stairs
and hides in plain sight.
I see it in seconds, rooting itself with the mirror
trying its best to be the worst kind of friend.
It tells jokes of deception,
of perfect angles and thighs that won't touch,
its glass eyes dancing in delight at
a constant suffering,
reflection of an irreversible desire to be less than.
Once again I am stuck inside walls
of self-built expectation and disgust,
praying to photoshop gods, but still all I see
is the addiction unraveling my skin,
a fever dream of starve and sculpt
and perfect never gets any closer.
It wakes me up and spends the morning
complaining about the cheap mattress,
the broken heating system screaming,
the light coming through the window.
It complains about my hungry cats and
already rumbling stomach, how *I just can't
seem to keep any of it away for long.*
It complains about this heavy and aching
body, never admitting how much wasting
away is still happening in this home.

Pathetic Wonderings

I don't care
what they say
in all of
the love songs,
all of the
pathetic croons about
the heart's miserable,
ridiculous ability to
ruin us. It
is not the
loving; that is
the best part
of it all.
The way she
held me through
the wandering nights,
the money spent
kindly and the
smeared lipstick all
over her face.
It was never
the good parts
that broke us,
but the wasting
away that happened
anyway, and left
us holding ourselves,
spent and smeared
and wondering alone.

Torches Burning

I fizzle at both ends.
Demands from the mirror
stay loud in a crowded skull.
There is burning here,
flames licking my lips,
the growing hunger merely
an inconvenience when I get
to look this small,
fractured in a reflection.
Still, I know I am dangerous to myself
Hopeless empty universe inside me,
there is no kindling here anymore.
I am a torch
a miracle
a surprise
that I may still wake up
with only oxygen keeping me alive.
Dehydrated current of motivation,
I may be doing my best but it is decidedly
not good enough to keep this hollow warm.

Maybe there is still enough time for me to get better,
to wash this away into a memory rather than a reality.

Panics, Still Awake

I know I've already locked the
    car outside
    front door (twice)
    garage door
    door at the top of the stairs
    back door
    windows,

but what if he's hiding in the
    closets
    bathrooms
    garage
    spare room?

I've already made a better home here,
but the ghost of a childhood robbed
by fear and eggshells makes me panic, still awake
wondering how far someone would go to keep
dirty hands fumbling for puppet strings
in a person he can no longer control

Two Visions

She came to me in a coffee shop-
There, against the wall with her

Best friends   Mother

Falling in love with my spotlight.
And I

Barely noticed her.   Noticed every move.

Our first date was shy,
Taking small

Bites   Sips

From things we bought ourselves.
For some reason, she made me crazy talking

Just enough. Months   Too much. Hours

Passed, and I knew how much
I wanted her. But life made

Her   Me

wait, until we were both ready,
until we were alone

Together.   Apart.

I didn't know how much I needed her
not then, until she

Stayed.   Left.

A barista sipping sunshine,
filling my nights with

Open wounds.   Phone calls.

We were just dizzy dreamers,
learning each other through the

Scars.   Distance.

Now, she washes her hands of me,
the way

I used to be.   She makes me scream.

It's always easier to breathe
when
She's not around.   She holds me.
Today I call her name,
and it becomes
An echo finally fading.   A synonym for home.

Since She Left

A stranger to apology,
to share that word between us,
to dare to breathe

                           sorry

but never quite say it out loud.
I think about missing her before remembering
the new love dancing with me into
comfort, settling easily. Again, I just
remember the chaos of us, the backs turned and
doors slammed and tears cried out and dried out.
The screaming and crying and gradual healing,
But still I call out in whispered silences
for closure to close this door on my own.

                i'm sorry i'm sorry i'm sorry
                  say it back please say it back.

but there is nothing left to be sorry for,
apology after poem written of the mess
long gone since she left: now a collage of
ceramic turtles and fading polaroids,
I write it all out of a bleeding heart
learning selfless love, a sigh of relief.
Still, I send her looks from across rooms, but

           look how much has happened since you left,
            how much of me is healing in the hollow of you,

but I can finally be okay that
nothing will ever   ever   ever
        be the same.

Always Fall In Love

Neither did I, think that I was
capable of recovering
in front of a mirror.
Such heavy proportions,
blown out in reflection and
dysmorphia, and maybe I never
saw things   or   said things
the same way I used to,
but there is a Ponderosa pine forest
in my backyard, and we always fall in love
dancing in our dusty backyard to the sound
of deer flicking their tails and turning their
keen snouts to the sound of peace,
of what is still to come like joy,
like family and moving right along,
the light swaying through trunks and branches
the way a wave rolls smoothly over the sky,
and maybe I am rooted, too, after all.
There is forgiveness growing here, how she
keeps coming back and calling me a home,
though I do still refuse to.
Though I am ever-empty,
I am learning the blessing that comes
with filling myself up with better things:
        her gentle three-squeeze hand in mine
        the *baby* at the edge of her lips
        sharing every lovable inch of me
        her fists against invisible demons
        the daisies that witness this big love
        our skin melting into the mattress

These poems, though maybe not always a lifeline,
                              are at least a reflection of living.
You could, at least, create a collage of me from them.
Every heartbeat that got me here are the threads
tying together a book that I will someday be lucky enough to
finish.

Lessons Still Coming

Maybe my mother doesn't know this,
but she is my favorite song: it goes like
I keep trying to visit in the summer but
instead I give her new names like
the slowest July I can remember and
a forgiving fever, we all broke so easily
in that house   didn't we?
Still can't come home to that hot silence.
Our hands gripped together sweat sticky
just clinging to a home cracked off the map
Now she screams and it is honey to me,
what a sweet mess, a serenade, a chaos

I am so glad that we are finally asking
questions of what we deserve,
lessons in a language of love on hot,
biting tongues. there is relief in
believing that we can have more.

My mother picks weeds in the yard and
buys herself flowers for the kitchen island.
she falls asleep in the cradle of a sweet
sherbet sunset, desert heart, the taste
of water in soil. Yes, mom, we can grow
again, just like before. there is bloom
in her laughter, in the scuffle and dance
of slippers on new hardwood. charges
into the day with open hands, and I
remember the way it all was before.
and I still keep coming home for more.

Rejected and Embraced

she reminds me how to be all howl
no body to deter the scream of joy
of anger burning quick and away
we have fought feral before and now
choose the harm less the ricochet
the ripple of broken bones and shock
factor in the wave of hurt it takes
to be that violent. it's all ash under
the rubble under a roof in flames,
anyway. now we lay in beds miles
apart and miss each other, keep tabs
on every social account just to feel
like we're finally connected, and
I know we both remember back when
the bobby pins were scattered in corners
along baseboards and one of us was
slamming cabinet doors. we were
climbing onto groaning counters
feet tucked under faucets sinking
into the harsh reflection of growing
up. out. in. toward each other.
here we go again, splashing into the
summer, deep blue eyes, the same nose.
this love, this *sister* once rejected from
my throat now a full embrace against
a shared trauma that did not kill us,
finding home in each other, in our
bodies full of forward, full of sun.

Leaving the Parties

we become
drunk lions
&
picture frames
&
dancing mirrors
&
flooded basements
&
life preservers
&
rattlesnakes
&
empty bars
&
warning signs
&
just one more
&
expected time
&
fading eyes
&
sloppy haircuts
&
slamming doors
&
fire escapes
&
spent emotion

Hollowed Me

Maybe once they might have considered
leaving me swinging from my own neck.
I used to love walking into parties and
proving myself to the sharpest shards of glass
eyes ready for the throat, an open cut the
warmest part of my unraveling. It's a thin
line sometimes, that precipice between
hollow and healing. Really, who would
have blamed them for watching me
drown in a million ways, sinking in the
white noise, blacked out. I mourn for
all the dying parts of me left rotting under
false spotlights, shining accidents, but
maybe now we are all becoming better
people, a little too late, but enough to
stay, to grow, to believe we are more
than the ways we auctioned ourselves off.

Meltdowns On

In the flight of mania I dance
with the empty and tumbling
boxes in my living room
grow out of another meltdown
and hold this fat heart up
to the light. Maybe I know that
big love isn't supposed to come
skinny and again I am grateful
for all the pain that led me here
to this moment, arms flailing out
to new favorite songs, jumping
onto the deep purple couch,
colliding with half full walls
and laughing with the ghosts of
past lives coming through the
air, bright yellow along the
carpet, and we are all still alive
and for once I am grateful
for all the pain that led them here
to this moment,
when I am alone
and dancing with the love
growing out of my feet
planting myself firmly into this
reality of letting the plants live
and letting myself live too
through all this ceramic memory,
all this fragile tissue paper
that barely holds me together.
Today I am still falling apart

you,
g how
ow out
ng along
fades for the stars.

Cracked Mirrors

have i
told you
about the
glass thrown
out? The
mirror finally
gone, a
girl in
new clothes
dancing to
her favorite
song and
knowing already
that she
is an
ocean of
beautiful, a
field of
meadows, a
full sunrise
growing over
this horizon
line, the
hardest part
gone as
time slows
down to
watch her
do nothing
but love.

Foggy Windows

What more is there
to say, girl, when
we are just strangers
that thought of love
when the light gleamed
and asked it to
be ours, let it
settle before uprooting again.
There are no more
words in my bones
for the way you
left me, for now
I'll be the one
to gladly say goodbye
as the fog in
the canyon rolls over
the highway, my windows
collecting every tear I
dared to waste on
someone whose heart wasn't
ever going to
be ready
for someone
like me.

Fading Ghosts

Another birthday passes and we eat confetti cupcakes on the
    kitchen floor,
much prefer the hardwood to the harsh light of height.

We drink the same pink wine from the grocery store in mason
    jar glasses
that made it unscathed through four moves away from a
    drowning desert home.

The ghosts made it through the tumbling wheels careening
    toward hope
in the form of new addresses, but even they are fading along
    with the candle smoke.

I never believed that I could outlast them, always assumed that
    I would
join their howling eventually, the way I used to crave
    evaporation.

But there is always a new season around the corner, and this
    one is
blooming like laughter in sparks against the dirty ceiling.

We are all itching to get out of here again, to chase the Arizona
    sunset
through meadows of cactus and Ponderosa and feel the wind
    wide open.

Somewhere else, another version of me still prays to a deaf
    universe,

keeps swallowing her own voice in favor of survival, and I am
   glad to have

outgrown her. Look how well I wear this color now. How the
   wave of
me keeps rolling, expanding into someone infinite and
   unbound and loved.

Increasingly Synthetic

I could not write when I was afraid,

though the night still tries to spill itself out:
     black ink on a page trapped by rough edges.

I press a still, unshaken hand to the mirror
and the collage of dying dreams falls away:

     a cardboard cutout,
     a crash test dummy,
     the cheap trick revealed
     the fake blood at
     the scene of a crime.

I hold the shards of loss in my open palms,
and these once desperate hopes feel false,
synthetic against the touch of growing health,

     of gratitude, that I am starting to find myself
     beyond the cheap cruelty of a reflection.

Big Eyes

And maybe now,
you will understand:

wherever you go becomes
a holy space, your eyes a
sacred moment, a big breath
I cannot catch, a love I will
worship for the rest of time,

Because
I love you
is all I can say
but never quite enough.

About Atmosphere Press

Atmosphere Press is an independent, full-service publisher for excellent books in all genres and for all audiences. Learn more about what we do at atmospherepress.com.

We encourage you to check out some of Atmosphere's latest releases, which are available at Amazon.com and via order from your local bookstore:

A Dream of Wide Water, poetry by Sharon Whitehill

Radical Dances of the Ferocious Kind, poetry by Tina Tru

The Woods Hold Us, poetry by Makani Speier-Brito

Report from the Sea of Moisture, poetry by Stuart Jay
    Silverman

The Enemy of Everything, poetry by Michael Jones

The Stargazers, poetry by James McKee

The Pretend Life, poetry by Michelle Brooks

Minnesota and Other Poems, poetry by Daniel N. Nelson

Interviews from the Last Days, sci-fi poetry by Christina
    Loraine

the oneness of Reality, poetry by Brock Mehler

About The Author

Kimberly Jarchow (she/they) is a queer poet from the desert currently pursuing an MFA in Creative Writing at Northern Arizona University in Flagstaff, Arizona. Her writing focuses on the struggles and joys that come with being queer, having mental illnesses, and overcoming trauma. In her free time she enjoys being in the mountains with her partner, snuggling with their two cats, and spending too much time in coffee shops.

CPSIA information can be obtained
at www.ICGtesting.com
Printed in the USA
LVHW051358041020
667875LV00003B/1205